Sewing Lessons

Judith A. Rypma

FUTURECYCLE PRESS

Mineral Bluff, Georgia

Published by FutureCycle Press
Mineral Bluff, Georgia, USA

ISBN 978-1-938853-26-5

Contents

I.

*She had not the slightest idea how
to spin straw into gold, and she became more and more
distressed, until at last she began to weep.*

—From "Rumpelstiltskin," The Brothers Grimm

Coffee Klatches in the Fifties

Wielding knitting needles
like dueling swords
neighbor ladies
clicked clacked
over mugs of Chase & Sanborn

destroying reputations
wasting lives

yarn serpents
dangling from laps
in a rainbow of colors
deceptive
as a coral snake
crawling across carpet

tempting little girls
into reaching for them

adding to the burden
we didn't yet know
Eve had already
picked for us.

Learning to Sew in the Sixties

It started with a 4-H towel:
ugly striped linen cloth

stitches slightly less crooked
on the stupid apron that followed

though we persevered. Coveted
ribbons never earned. Moved on

to ripping out bad hems, unsticking
zippers, separating sleeves threaded

together. By our teens past caring
about winning. Just desperate

to pass Home Ec. Crying over
the crinkled velvet disaster originally

destined for a homecoming dance.
Soon after finding new uses for

needles. Draping necks with beads.
Torching those damned latex bras.

No clue some of us were burning
the fabric of our futures.

The Singer

Grew up hating
that machine:
black curse
in every woman's home.

Foot pedals
intended to stop and start
stitch and hem
make cloth music.

Probably how the manufacturer
came up with that name
though I fumbled
each time I touched it
failed to carry a tune.

Pricked fingers.
Sewed legs to arms
zippers to hems
precursor
to the discord:

silks and satins
I'd never own
baby clothes
never needed
lullabies unsung

high notes
I'd never reach.

Impossible Tasks

Growing up we braided
everything:
each other's hair
potholder loops
dandelion stems
plastic purses, key chains

eventually gave up
threading, stringing, plaiting

for weaving
long-term connections

realizing only after
multiple tangled tries
that no temper tantrum
by a grumpy dwarf

could transform
strands of our future.

That we would never
learn to spin

straw of our lives
into gold.

From Ariadne: 4 A.M.

Dammit. Middle of a night
cool as that kiss
before his transport left

wondering why
the king still sends youths
as a sacrifice

though hers seemed so eager
to lift anchor. Replaying
every word he said
or didn't. Pondering
why his gear contained
a childhood train set
photo of him in dress whites
sweater his mother knitted

as if he planned
on never returning
or perhaps sailing off
to another port
if he survived.

Somewhere there's a thread
she needs to follow
but Theseus has taken the spool

abandoning her
in the national labyrinth
while he goes off to fight
a Minotaur
leaving her to wrestle monsters
waging war in her head.

Pulling Stitches

A life, too
can be explicated —

pulling, unraveling
darning, stitching

thin threads that connect us
hems that rise and fall

sag, fray
if you make too many errors

use the wrong fabric
pick a poor pattern.

Yearning

Some of us still
possess four thumbs
cannot tie a knot
sew on a button
create a straight seam

perceive no difference
between knit, purl
silk, satin
velvet, Velcro
linen, lace.

Instead struggle
with past or present tense
first or third person

quilted sentences
scraps
of odd-sized ideas

occasional masterpieces
no one may ever see.

Coming Apart

No one really knows
if you've used a safety pin
or Scotch tape
to stop seams from unraveling
keep it all together

or those bitter pills
with x's in their names
promising
to make life appear
good as new

hide flaws
of your unzipped brain.

Sewing Lessons

A hem attached to a sleeve
in Home Ec class.
Snow White's mother
failing to seek
needle puncture treatment.

Arachne too good a job.
Sleeping Beauty overcome
by spinning wheel curiosity
sacrificing a century
for a man.

Ah, who hasn't
pricked a finger, slept
through life's best parts
loosened
every last stitch.

II.

...the distaff and spindle are such an intrinsic part of a woman's life that they are often buried with her.

—from *The Northmen* by Thomas Froncek

Webs

E. B. White started it
letting Charlotte spin phrases
transforming Wilbur into

a media darling
while each day she repaired holes
mended, revised

while he won prizes
until she weakened
called the sac she made

her *magnum opus.*
Did not live to see
what she left behind

because that is what we do—
even females devoting last days
to spinning tales.

Dressing in the Sixties

First the pleated skirts
hours of starching
to align them perfectly beneath
ruffled blouses with tight collars

layers of petticoats blown up
with a tube
so they'd rustle loudly
transform us into puffy Southern belles.

Eventually we bought girdles
fastened nylons
with dangling plastic loops
that indented backs of thighs

replaced clunky saddle shoes
with glittering penny loafers
pierced heads with bobby pins
driven through fat rollers
or baby curls
then plastic headbands with teeth
chewing into ironed hair.

Later we tossed everything out—
ear-pinching clip-ons,
all the spandex, garter belts, bras.
Gleefully chopped hair.
Embraced fishnets, panty hose
then kilts, midis, minis
sandals, jeans, pea coats.

Kept only precious shadows,
liners, glosses, polishes. Excitement
of a box of 64 Crayolas.

Imagined then
we were moving on
to looser, freer lives

failed to envision
decades and decades
of constrictions
that would follow.

Weaving Woman

> ...when a Huichol woman is about to weave or embroider,
> her husband catches a large serpent and holds it in a cleft
> stick, while the woman strokes the reptile with one hand
> down the whole length of its back; then she passes the same
> hand over her forehead and eyes, that she may be able to
> work as beautiful patterns in the web as the markings on
> the back of the serpent.

—Sir James Frazer, *The Golden Bough*

I consider killing a spider scurrying over my notes
but cannot. Perhaps she has her own manuscript
webbed across book spines we share.
She's the weaver I've never been.

It started in grade school: five nails
and an empty spool, friends creating
knitted tubes that grew and grew
while mine evolved into
a stunted yarn snake.
Weaving nylon loops into potholders: in
and out, out and in, across, down, over, under
no possibility of error except for my
odd diagonals, asymmetrical squares.

Get thee from me, Despair.
I have no fig leaves to protect a naked mind.
Thou sewest up mine iniquity.

I'm no Dorcas. Will never exhibit
ribbons, kudos, awards, contracts
eliciting Athena's envy—no risk
she'll destroy this word fabric, pity
a grieving woman

though she might yet choose
to transform the rope into
a perfect silk strand from which I can dangle

with this Arachne seeking refuge
beneath my papers. By sunrise
I've faced down the serpent,
returned to the loom, fingers pressed to
the anguished forehead where I pray
intricate tracery awaits. Know only
I will live
to weave
at least one more day.

Obsession

Another sleepless night. Wasted.
Alone
         hooking words
across, up, down
colorless pages

beginning to comprehend
Spider Woman's compulsion
to weave
herself into
a desert sand blanket

hoping
for her waning strength
         to create a spirit thread
to follow out
of myself.

The Spoils of Death

Sifting through her things I am a voyeur
spying on memories — a thief

stealing a life. Can't accept
the trade: one silver tea service, crystal

salt and pepper shakers, jade beads
she wore Sundays, nineteenth-century lamp

hand-painted with chrysanthemums
collection of hand-woven potholders

items admired, coveted for decades
exchanged for her absence

as if possession means
antiques, china, jewels, cash

letters I wasn't meant to read
consolation prizes not earned

awarded by default for living
longest. Trinkets you'd trade back

for time — the only thing
truly worth owning.

Hanging On

At the window, rocking
she folds
into herself. Stares at
dappled hands no one wants
to hold now. Struggles
to recapture ideas

evaporating quickly as rain
but refusing
to condense heavenward
drift down later to nourish
a parched recollection.

That man — no face
but a scent of musk

bending to offer
peppermint tea, wrapped gift.
Planting a rose petal kiss
on her brow. He whispers
something about
a weekend in Budapest

and is gone

leaving her wrapped
in an afghan she might've knitted

murmuring
to a wet reflection.

It happens the same way
in her dreams. Vivid

burly shapes
she can almost touch

lovers dancing
in her head

stroking once again silky skin
worshipping subtle limbs
her fine-tuned mind.

New sleep clouds rumble in
webbed fingers shoving aside
happiness, gauzing memories

until they shred
dissipate into wool fog

when she awakens
groggy and alone
clutching at the afghan

reaching for someone who
before the first cup of coffee
will have abandoned her.

Baling

I'd pay top dollar
for an ounce
of anything
that sheds years
sweetens memories:
eau de clover
or alfalfa water —
aroma whisking me back

to afternoons saturated
with promise.
Hair still the color
of ripened wheat
limbs strong for straddling
the wagon's summit
as it wobbled sunrise to sunset

teeth
hard, white pearls
chewing straw strands
seeking, finding
unrecognized fodder
for a youth filled
with important duties

like constructing camps
in the loft where we stacked bales
toasted in golden loaves
wrapped in twine ribbons —

gifts for our future
we took for granted

while nimbly scrambling
through quilted farms
and up hay mountains

that fed our souls
with the bread of youth.

Sewing Ladies

The Three Fates
may have controlled life's threads
but one way or another
Circe, Calypso, Arachne, Helen
all lost
the sewing game—
belly-spun fibers
another way to deal with loss

or Penelope threading, unthreading
the same shroud
probably wishing a million times
to be buried in it
rather than devote life
to waiting.

or the Lady of Shalott
abandoning her tower
for quilted fields
and a worthless knight.
Trading the loom
for an early demise.

Oh, eight-legged Satan
and Savior. Hindu weaver
of illusion: do not hide
truth
or let me
meticulously construct this web
that will inevitably entrap me.

Instead reveal
which goddess, spirit, muse
I should serve tonight

and how much sacrifice
will be required.

Amber Spindles

Baltic ancients placed them
in women's graves

laid matching honeyed discs
on closed eyelids

recognizing links
between sun, spinning, fate

more permanent prayers
to the golden Sun Goddess

who guaranteed new thread
from the earth. A chance

to avoid unhappiness
repeat of life's darkness.

They must've buried me
again and again

but without amber
no protection

from malicious spirits.
Until last time

when someone
slipped it beside the body

so that I'm finally certain
light's rays are splintering

in straight lines. Not snarling
or tangling in heavens above me.

Connections

So many patterns
written in sky —
shredded fibers
pulling together into
robust cotton clouds.
Butterflies flitting from one waving blossom
to the next. Geese
tracing the alphabet
in formation.
Snowflakes
reassembling
into the plow's white stacks

the mountains themselves —
connected triangular peaks
stitching valleys, steering
storms, humbling travelers
beneath constellations
of precisely placed stars.

We could follow them all
use their ancient maps
to guide loose souls
find our place
in Pope's stupendous whole.

Acknowledgments

Thanks to the following publications, in which some of these poems first appeared:

Haight Ashbury Literary Journal: "From Ariadne: 4 A.M."
Nimrod: "Weaving Woman"
Oracle: "Webs"
Pearl: "Sewing Lessons"
Pegasus Review: "Connections"
Puerto del Sol: "The Spoils of Death"
Red Wheelbarrow: "Hanging On"
Wayne Literary Review: "Baling"

Cover art, "Sien, Sitting on a Basket, with a Girl," by Vincent Van Gogh; author photo courtesy of Western Michigan University; cover and interior book design by Diane Kistner (dkistner@futurecycle.org); Book Antiqua text with Cronos SemiBold titling

About FutureCycle Press

FutureCycle Press is dedicated to publishing lasting English-language poetry and flash fiction books, chapbooks, and anthologies in both print-on-demand and ebook formats. Founded in 2007 by long-time independent editor/publishers and partners Diane Kistner and Robert S. King, the press incorporated as a nonprofit in 2012. A number of our editors are distinguished poets and authors in their own right, and we have been actively involved in the small press movement going back to the early seventies.

The FutureCycle Poetry Book Prize and honorarium is awarded annually for the best full-length volume of poetry we publish in a calendar year. Introduced in 2013, our Good Works projects are devoted to issues of global significance, with all proceeds donated to a related worthy cause. We are dedicated to giving all authors we publish the care their work deserves, making our catalog of titles the most distinguished it can be, and paying forward any earnings to fund more great books.

We've learned a few things about independent publishing over the years. We've also evolved a unique, resilient publishing model that allows us to focus mainly on vetting and preserving for posterity the most books of exceptional quality without becoming overwhelmed with bookkeeping and mailing, fundraising activities, or taxing editorial and production "bubbles." To find out more about what we are doing, come see us at www.futurecycle.org.

www.ingramcontent.com/pod-product-compliance
Lightning Source LLC
Chambersburg PA
CBHW061200040426
42445CB00013B/1761